John Joubert
Carols & Anthems

The Novello Choral Programme

Novello Publishing Limited
(A division of Music Sales Limited)
8/9 Frith Street, London W1D 3JB, England

Novello

NOV200216
ISBN No. 0-7119-8480-8

Music setting by Barnes Music Engraving
Cover design by Michael Bell Design
Cover picture by Frank Gresham

This edition © 2000 Novello Publishing Limited
Published in Great Britain by Novello Publishing Limited

Head office: 8/9, Frith Street, London W1D 3JB, England

Telephone: +44 (0)20 7434 0066
Fax: +44 (0)20 7287 6329

Sales and hire:
Music Sales Limited,
Newmarket Road, Bury St. Edmunds, Suffolk IP33 3YB

www.musicsales.com

e-mail: music@musicsales.co.uk

John Joubert was born in Cape Town in 1927 and educated at the Diocesan College in Rondebosch where he came under the guidance of the musical director Claude Brown, whose teaching he regarded as "an indispensable foundation to my subsequent musical career". Through his teacher's encouragement, Joubert was able to participate in choral performances with the Cape Town Municipal Orchestra under William J. Pickerill and subsequently to hear his works featured in performance. The greatest influence on his composition, however, was William Henry Bell, an English-born composer who taught Joubert privately following his graduation from the South African College of Music in 1944.

The following year, Joubert was awarded a Performing Right Society Scholarship to study at the Royal Academy of Music in London, where he studied with Theodore Holland, Howard Ferguson and Alan Bush. He was recipient of a Royal Philharmonic Prize in 1949, took up a music lectureship at Hull University in 1950 and in 1952 won the Novello Anthem Competition with his *O Lorde, the maker of al thing*. In 1962 he was appointed Senior Lecturer and subsequently Reader in Music at the University of Birmingham and, following early retirement, was appointed Senior Research Fellow at Birmingham in 1997. He is also an honorary Doctor of Music at Durham University. He has received commissions from Three Choirs and Birmingham Triennial Festivals, from the City of Birmingham Symphony Orchestra, the Royal Philharmonic Society and the BBC.

Among his many often large scale works are two symphonies, concertos for violin, piano and bassoon, seven operas, many large scale choral works, a number of instrumental and small ensemble and vocal pieces. His instinctive feel for literature is evident in operas like *Silas Marner* (George Eliot), *Under Western Eyes* (Conrad) or *Jane Eyre* (Charlotte Brontë) or smaller settings of poets like Lawrence *(The Instant Moment)*, Hardy *(South of the Line)* or Mandelstam *(Tristia)*. He is most widely known and appreciated for his prodigious gifts as composer of short choral works, mostly to liturgical or other Christian texts, with or without instrumental accompaniment, including the world famous carols *Torches* (1951) and *There is no rose* (1954), as well as the more sustained *Rorate coeli* (1985). In all of these, mastery of materials is put to the creation of work that is of deceptive and utter simplicity.

This Anthem won first prize in the Novello Anthem Competition, 1952

O Lorde, the maker of al thing

Anthem for S.A.T.B. and Organ

Words:
King Henry VIII

JOHN JOUBERT, op. 7b

4

There is no rose of such virtue

Carol for S.A.T.B. (unaccompanied)

Words:
Medieval

JOHN JOUBERT, op. 14

For in this rose con - tain - èd was Heav'n and earth in

For in this rose con - tain - èd was Heav'n and earth in

For in this rose con - tain - èd was Heav'n and earth in

For in this rose con - tain - èd was Heav'n and earth in

lit - tle space: Res_____ mi-ran - da.

lit - tle space: Res_____ mi-ran - da.

lit - tle space: Res_____ mi - ran - da.

lit - tle space: Res_____ mi - ran - da.

For the Choir of St. Paul's Church, Westfield, New Jersey, USA

Christ is risen

Anthem for S.A.T.B. and Organ

Words:
I Corinthians 15, v. 20

JOHN JOUBERT, op. 36

Commissioned by the Rev Dr P. C. Moore for the choir of Pershore Abbey
To my Mother

The Beatitudes

Anthem for S. T. Soli and S.A.T.B. (unaccompanied)

Words:
St Matthew 5, vv. 3–12

JOHN JOUBERT, op. 47

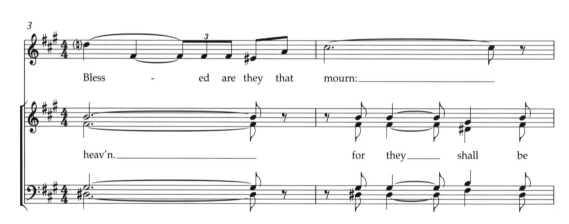

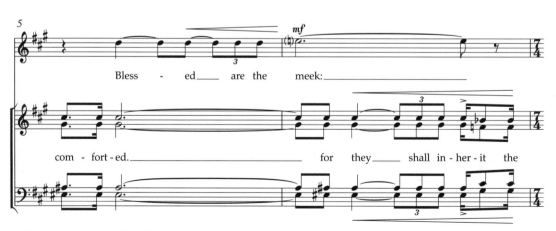

O praise God in his holiness

Anthem for S.A.T.B. and Organ

Words:
Psalm 150

JOHN JOUBERT, op. 52

of his pow'r.

Praise_ him in his no - ble acts:_

praise him ac - cord - ing to his ex - cel - lent

great - ness._____ Praise__ him in the sound of the

trum - pet:_____ praise him up-on the

lute_____ and____ harp._____

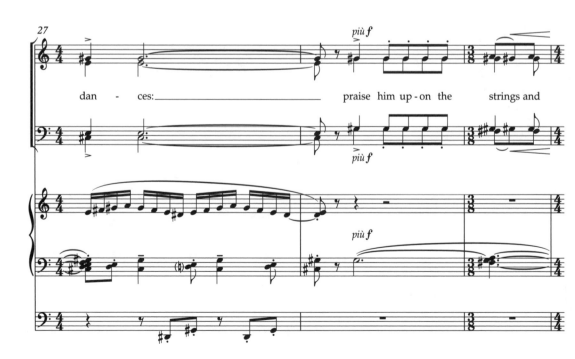

pipe._____ Praise him up-on the well - tuned

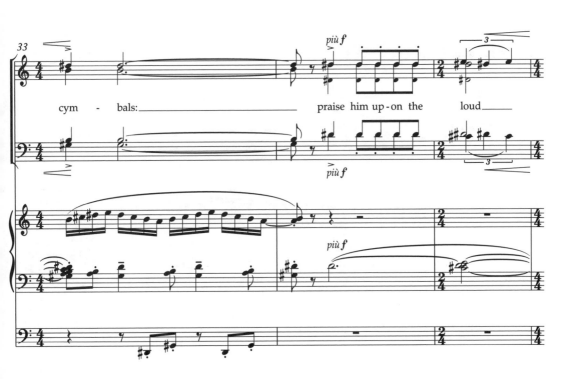

cym - bals:_____ praise him up-on the loud____

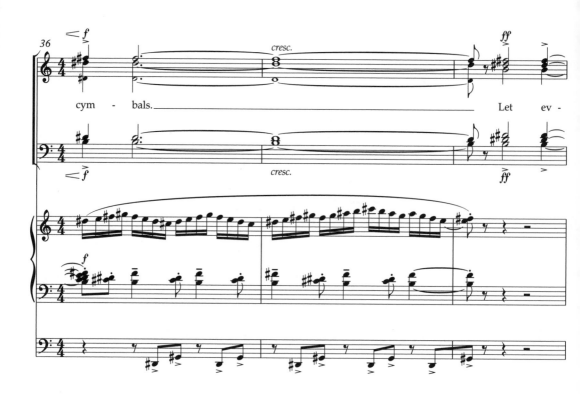

cym - bals. Let ev -

- 'ry-thing that hath breath: praise,

praise,_____ praise_____ the___

Lord._____

Specially composed for the Festival of St. Cecilia, 1967

Lord, thou hast been our refuge

Anthem for S.A.T.B. and Organ

Words:
Psalm 90 (vv. 1–7, 9, 13, 17)

JOHN JOUBERT, op. 53

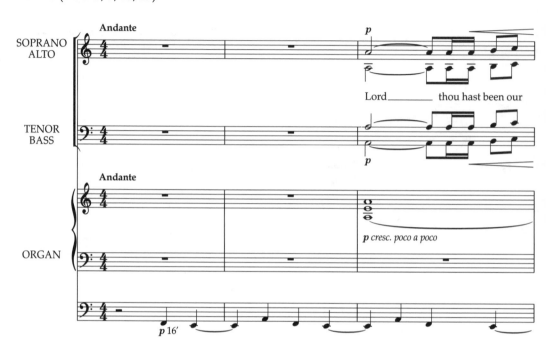

Be-fore the moun-tains were brought forth,__ or ev-er the earth and the world were made:

thou art God from ev-er-last-ing, and world with-out__ end.

BASS SOLO

Thou turn-est man to de-struc-tion: a - gain__ thou say -

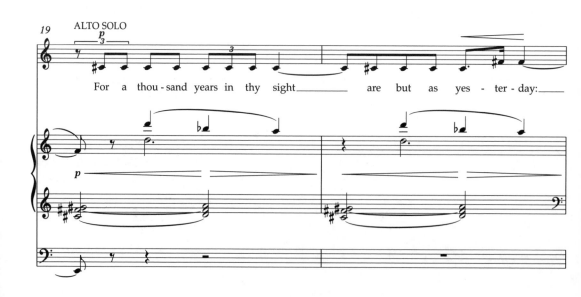

All and some
(Nowell sing we)

Carol for S.A.T.B. and Organ

Words:
15th century (adapted)

JOHN JOUBERT, op. 58

* The small notes before the beat

Words from Musica Brittanica Vol. 4 by permission of the Royal Musical Association

As sun-ne shin-eth through the glass,___

So Je-su in his mo-ther was;___

Thee to ser-ve now grant us grace, thee to ser-ve now grant us grace,___

Commissioned by St Michael's College, Tenbury

Coverdale's Carol

for S.A.T.B. (unaccompanied)

Words:
Miles Coverdale (1457–1568)

JOHN JOUBERT, op. 75

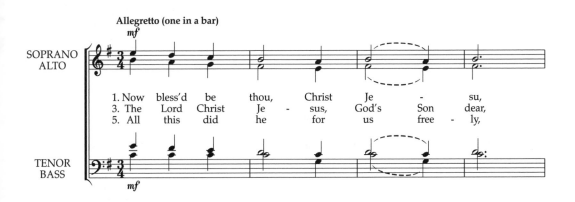

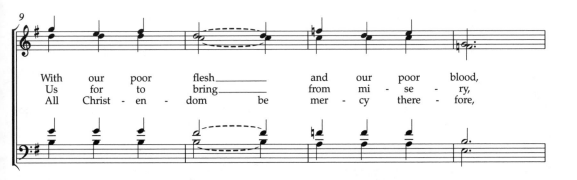

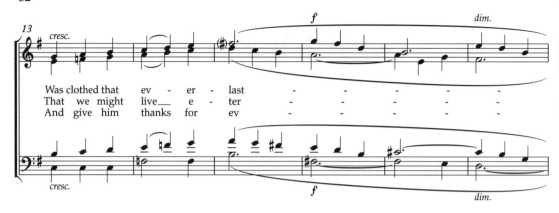

Was clothed that ev - er - last - - - - -
That we might live__ e - ter - - - - -
And give him thanks for ev - - - - -

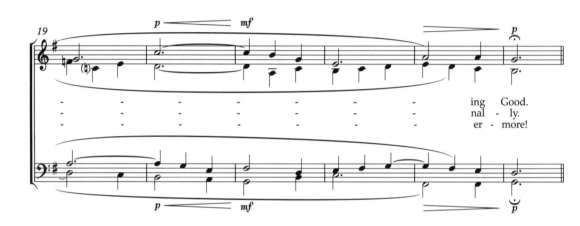

- - - - - - - ing Good.
- - - - - - - nal - ly.
- - - - - - - er - more!

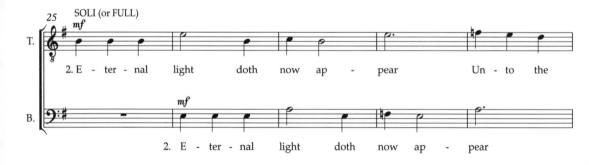

SOLI (or FULL)

T.

2. E - ter - nal light doth now ap - pear Un - to the

B.

2. E - ter - nal light doth now ap - pear

world both far and near; It shin - eth clear

Un - to the world both far and near; It shin - eth

e - ven at mid - night, Mak - ing us chil - -

clear e - ven at mid - night, Mak - ing us chil -

- - - - dren,_____ chil -

- - - - - - dren,_____

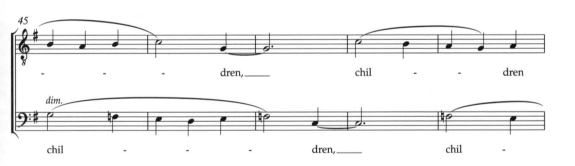

- - - dren,_____ chil - - dren

chil - - - dren,_____ chil -

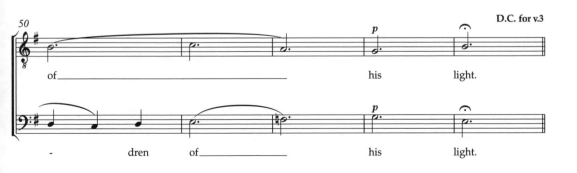

D.C. for v.3

of_____ his light.

- dren of_____ his light.

Hymn to the Virgin

Carol for S.S. soli and S.A.T.B. (unaccompanied)

Words:
Old English

JOHN JOUBERT, op. 102

Words from the *Oxford Book of English Verse* by permission of Oxford University Press.

56

Commissioned for the centenary of the Exeter Diocesan Choral Association 1986
For Lucian Nethsingha

Glory and honour

Anthem for S.A.T.B. and Organ

Words:
The Alternative Service Book 1980

JOHN JOUBERT, op. 106

The canticle 'Glory and Honour' from Evening Prayer in the Alternative Service Book 1980 derives from the Daily Office of the Joint Liturgical Group, and is reproduced by permission of the Central Board of Finance of the Church of England.

and hon - our and power:_____

and hon - our and power:_____

and hon - our and power:_____

and hon - our and power:_____

are yours by right,_____

are yours by right,_____

are yours by right,_____

are yours by right,_____

be - fore our God.

be - fore our God.

be - fore our God.

be - fore our God.

Tempo I (←♩ = ♩→)

70

Commissioned by Peter Bennett, and dedicated to Mrs. B. Bennett and the Sheffield Chorale

The Christ-child lay

Carol for S.A.T.B. (unaccompanied)

Words:
G. K. Chesterton (1874–1936)

JOHN JOUBERT, op. 136a

Words reproduced by permission of A. P. Watt Limited on behalf of the Royal Literary Fund.

17

His hair_ was like_ a fire.____ (O

Christ-child lay_ on Ma - ry's heart,____ His hair_ was like_ a fire.____ (O

21

wear - y, wear - y is__ the world,____ But here_ the world's de - sire.)____ The

wear - y, wear - y is__ the world,____ But here the world's de - sire.)____ The

wear - y, wear - y is__ the world,____ But here the world's de - sire.)____ The

wear - y, wear - y is__ the world,____ But here the world's de - sire.)____ The

In memory of H.A. Joubert, O.D., and of Joan Joubert (née Silberbauer)

The Souls of the Righteous

Anthem for S.A.T.B. and Organ

Words:
The Wisdom of Solomon Ch.3, vv.1–3

JOHN JOUBERT, op. 142

84

peace, —
peace, —
peace,
peace, —

rit.   molto lento

in peace.
in peace.
in peace.
in peace.

rit.   molto lento

Printed and bound in Great Britain by Caligraving Limited

Music origination by
Barnes Music Engraving Ltd, East Sussex